Blood at the Root

poems by

Latorial Faison

Finishing Line Press
Georgetown, Kentucky

Blood at the Root

to the ones who bear witness

—lf

Copyright © 2025 by Latorial Faison
ISBN 979-8-89990-250-5 First Edition
All rights reserved under International and Pan-American Copyright Conventions. No part of this book may be reproduced in any manner whatsoever without written permission from the publisher, except in the case of brief quotations embodied in critical articles and reviews.

ACKNOWLEDGMENTS

Many thanks to the editors of the following literary publications in which the following poems have appeared, some in earlier versions:

"America," *Poetry SuperHighway*
"Black Boys," *About Place Journal*
"My Blackness," *Black Girl Seeks*
"This," *The Watering Hole*
"This Religion," *OF ZOOS, Poetry Superhighway*
"Citizens" *Solstice Literary Magazine*

"Zip Code: 75215" as "Judas Kiss," *Artemis Journal*
"Haiku for My Ancestors" as "Sundays," *Aunt Chloe*
"If We Perish" as "Testify," Pushcart Nominee, *West Trestle Review*
"Down the Red Road" as "This Burden of Strange Fruit," *The Chattahoochee Review*
"Hidden Figures" as "Look, America," *Black Girl Seeks*
"Birthing Blackness" as "What He Gave," *Poetry Quarterly*
"Black Friday" as "Troubled Water," *Cultural Front #BlackPoetsSpeakOut*

"When Black Lives Mattered," as "Hallelujah Anyhow" *Aunt Chloe*
"Stars of Wonder" as "Nursery Rhyme in Black," *RHINO*, Founders Prize *Finalist*
"Mama Was a Negro Spiritual," *Southern Poetry Anthology: IX*
    Winning Writers Tom Howard Poetry Prize
    Furious Flower Inaugural Gwendolyn Brooks Prize Semifinalist
"Mama Sang the Blues," *PENUMBRA*
"How to Bury Your Mama," *Typehouse Literary Journal*

Publisher: Leah Huete de Maines
Editor: Christen Kincaid
Cover Art: *Homecoming, Virginia State University* by Latorial Faison
Author Photo: Latorial Faison
Cover Design: Elizabeth Maines McCleavy

Order online: www.finishinglinepress.com
Also available on amazon.com

Author inquiries and mail orders:
Finishing Line Press
PO Box 1626
Georgetown, Kentucky 40324
USA

Contents

Citizens	1
This	2
Blackness	3
Warmongers	4
If We Must Die	5
Black Friday	6
Our Declaration	7
Undocumented	8
If We Perish	9
When Black Lives Mattered	10
Mama Sang the Blues	11
A Couple of Forevers	13
Losing It	14
A Eulogy for America's Black Boy	15
Asunder	17
You People	18
Freedom Ride	19
Ritual Combat	20
I Am Not Ashamed of Your Gospel	21
To Black Fire	22
This Religion	23
Birthing Blackness	24
With All This Freedom	25
My Blackness	26
Disappearing Black	27
Abomination(s)	28
Simple Sentences	29
Mama Was a Negro Spiritual	30
Black Boys	32

Profiled	33
Birth of a Sensation	34
Primary Colors	35
What We Might Have Been	36
Here in the Darkness	37
Hidden Figures	38
Left Behind	39
Exegesis	40
Down the Red Road	41
Intersections	42
They Don't Give a Damn About Us	43
You Who Stand	45
Help My Unbelief	46
Columbus, Half-mast	47
Mirrors	48
She Who Gives Love	49
The Invocation	50
What Fools Want	51
Haiku for My Ancestors	52
Pledging	53
Strong as a Freedom Song	54
Job 1-21	55
Eulogy for Nat Turner	58
Castrated	61
Salt	62
How to Bury Your Mama	63
Stars of Wonder	65
Zip Code: 75215	66
America	67
Legend of Southampton County	68

Introduction

I grew up in rural Southampton County, Virginia, a place both ordinary and extraordinary. I was raised by my grandparents, people of humble beginnings whose hands and faith carried them through a world that was not always kind to them, but who made a way for me.

Southampton County is where I learned the weight of history. It is land remembered for slavery and survival, for cotton fields and church pews, for hard work and hope. It is where Nat Turner led one of the most powerful revolts against slavery in American history. To grow up in that place meant growing up with the echoes of struggle and the songs of resilience.

This book is born out of that inheritance. It is shaped by the voices of my ancestors, by the faith of my grandparents, and by the realities of being Black in America. The poems speak to what it means to live with memory, to carry grief, and yet to still rise with joy and determination.

Blood at the Root is not just my story. It is our story. It is the story of Black lives—how we have been erased, how we have endured, and how we continue to create beauty and truth in the face of injustice.

I hope these poems bring you closer to that truth, and I hope they remind you, as they remind me, that even in the most difficult places, there is still life even when blood is at the root.

—Latorial Faison, EdD

Citizens

Some were perched on the limbs of D.C. trees to get a glimpse of it, history being made, once again, in the angst of all the black & white, to hear Aretha spin her rhythm & blues into a hymn where hymns had never been made, up close, on a jumbotron, in the nation's capital. All that colored hope collected on white ballots, dreamed on Jim Crow nights & birthed in the belly of a red, white & blue sale, hope stolen off the coast of Africa, hope chained to a tree in Florida, hope purchased at a Galveston, Texas auction block, hope sold down a river in Charleston, hope traded for a racehorse in Missouri, hope terrorized by white hoods in Alabama, hope raped in Georgia, hope lynched & mutilated at the age of fourteen in Mississippi, hope assassinated on a balcony in Tennessee, hope in a Virginia slave preacher's revolt, hope from the Carolinas to the sandy shores of Maryland. We came to hold this truth to be self-evident that *all* Negroes are created equal to the forty-fourth President of the United States of America.

This

This un-blue blood in darker skin, this youth & manhood trapped within. This un-grown seed beset with doom, this unknown soul locked up, entombed. This brown face, this topless bottom, this man-child approaching Sodom. This buried chest of un-cried tears, this proverb unspoken through the years. This dissonant experience, this scent of crime for innocence. This shoot-to-kill with both hands up, this birthright linking chains & cuffs. This country's witness to its hate, this issue framed without debate. This urban trend & country woe, this poison root we plant & grow. This history we cannot bear, this melting pot we cannot share. This nightmare that we know is real, this voiceless blackness slaughtered still.

Blackness

for Langston Hughes

   Let go of blackness,
wear it in a suit.
   Boy if you don't,
here folks will shoot.

Let go of blackness,
   speak nice & white.
Child if you don't,
   you may have to fight.

   Let go of blackness,
don't let it show,
   or hate & prejudice
is all you may know.

   Let go of blackness,
for when blackness dies,
   nobody here cares.
nobody here cries.

Warmongers

This blood & these psychopaths—
        we do not mix our poisons well.
We have chased this shame with too many dilemmas:
        politics, money, media, silence.
In this shade & that—
        they have come layering our fear,
        saturating our pain,
        camouflaging what so historically has come
        to change us,
        to charge us with this chaos we carry.
Like rape babies in dying wombs,
Like martyred queens alive in tombs,
        we cannot live—
        except we declare this war.

If We Must Die

for Claude McKay

       If we still must die
           like roadkill
    on each side the Mason Dixon Line
         like a Till whistle
           blown
through a Southern breeze
    like a young buck
   black & running
     fighting
       killing
            writing
for our lives
        —like our Black lives—
matter
         then let us
           bleed
                and tell the story
   of these bullets
        between our eyes.

Black Friday

In this big, white tub soaking all this brown
        to loud deafening silence.

Amid all the world's chaos & noise,
        all of Washington's politically complex poise,
You are still the dream,
        still the hope of America's slave.

And while this pot is daily stirred,
        while it boils & spills the blood of hope
        —for our future—
Come, wade in this troubled water with me.
Come clean in the precious blood of our lambs.

Our Declaration

We have felt these words
like American butchers' knives
cutting us up & down
our hand-me-down American
seams
Reincarnating US—
Men, women & children
without legs to walk
without voice to talk
without hands to hold
fast
to a dream
our country
wears
upon a mask,
hides
beneath a robe,
speaks
into existence
with the lies
of a Constitution.

Undocumented

      I am African.
I am American.
         I am not anybody
Anybody can trace.

If We Perish

Would somebody help me count the blessing,
come forward—
        to see the violence,
        to say that it is real?

It is the saddest funeral,
these are the worst of times,
        and we look so happy
        dying.

When Black Lives Mattered

Mama drove a yellow school bus, cooked in school cafeterias & cleaned white folk's houses. Daddy cleaned their yards, worked their farms, drove nails in their boards, built their houses, their schools, their churches, their office buildings, their grocery & department stores. They came home every day to a four-turned-eight room house that took over thirty years to pay for, the house for which they worked hard to make a home—for me & every child who laid their head down in it, every child they raised, every moment they gave for somebody else. They knew Black America like the backs of their hands, that it was a 'Hallelujah' anyhow, that it was a dice game, a juke joint, a song they danced, a 'come to Jesus' moment; it was more than what they had yesterday. It was scattered with hope for what a tomorrow could bring. They knew white America was no Black man's promised land. But they got out of bed every day anyhow, pressed on for whatever victory they had in that white Jesus hanging high in a picture framed in their living room. Even he looked up, so they kept the faith because in America, life could change for the better in a hot-as-hell minute, in a marriage, in a child's birth, in a funeral, in a graduation, in a white woman's kitchen, or in the tilling of a white man's field. There rested a promise that hard work paid, not well, but good enough to raise boys & girls America might one day call sons and daughters, men & women, black or white, rich or poor, American. Black lives mattered to them, to them first, to them foremost, to them most of all.

Mama Sang the Blues

I.

Mama's bottle tested illusion. Therein was holy water from a great river that healed the sick and raised the dead. She sipped small sips with her black lips, hummed hymns nice and slow, in and out of contralto, like Mahalia Jackson. "Tell the angels," she'd sing—"I'm on my way," toe-tapping, head-rocking, hardworking, poor, and saved. Bittersweet like a one-room school, she came together without academic tools; she was heaven sent. The god of white evil couldn't create a Black woman like this. Like a day star, she appeared in indigo skies, orphaned and unknown. From a dying womb to a tenant room, she came like a blonde-haired, blue-eyed baby Jesus in a brown skinned country—it didn't make no sense. The poison she picked, it was a balm that chased evil, from lying tongues to the lynching of sons. Mama grew stronger than Samson on a Friday night when she slipped away to steal her humanity back. It was a happy sadness that dealt in pain, one I never heard her name or give claim. For when the white folk got your tongue, you can't talk to nobody but Jesus, and when Jesus got you singing like Mahalia, you can't trust nobody but God.

Mama Sang the Blues

II.

Mama was serious about religion, the Baptist church down the dirt road, and choir rehearsals on Tuesday nights. With song books, handwritten lyrics, and a third grade education, she impressed her own self. Standing in that choir on the promises of God, all robed and righteous, she was worth more than white women. Her voice, like a whippoorwill, could whistle and sing all through the night, all through the struggle, all through the pain, all through the blackness of being dead and alive. When she sang from her darkness, I knew she was light. Mama was a voice of dark brown reason—calling out to god, crying out from Earth. "What can wash away my sin, what can make me whole again . . ." I listened with everything that had come between us. She helped turn me into me with a melody she had sewn together through all kinds of hell. "O precious is thy flow that makes me white as snow . . ." Mama was an instrument inhaling grief, exhaling peace of mind, a piece of mine. She was a professor of arts and letters and god quilting me with all the pieces she was. Like whippoorwills, like Mama, and like every strong Black woman who came before me, I "come to this fountain . . . rich and sweet." They come whistling. She comes singing. I come believing that we come to raise the dead.

A Couple of Forevers

Thirty years of us lie
        trapped in two words
        globed by a submerging discourse.
It's clear to us now
        clear as crystal
        crystal as the wine glasses gifted us on our wedding day.
We thought
        We would stay the same.
We thought
        we would be different
We thought
        we would be
forever.

Losing It

      It came for us, dressed in apprehension,
sitting outside a spring revival
      upon an old mourner's bench,
chasing a dead woman's scream.

      Our light & dark mothers climbed
down a magnolia tree
      while we sipped from the drinking gourd
sweetening to taste—this freedom.

A Eulogy for America's Black Boy

Every night I bury him in a casket like Michael's
Because he is a prince the world neither knows nor understands—

>his genius undiscovered
>his beauty not yet born
>his blackness all too familiar
>his brothers alive yet invisible
>his mom, Black feminism refuted
>his father, another red flag saluted.

Each night I lower him down.
I let go of pieces of him
That shy shine in his eyes,
Un-laughable laughter, charm for charisma
His swagger is in his heartbeat
The drum beat of the man-child I bore.

Every night I bury so much dead
Sorrow from all his frustration,
An angst that comes with his miseducation
The pain & suffering of this birth,
Each miscalculated ounce of his self-worth
Everything that went wrong
I remember right here.

In this bed where sleep won't come
I say a prayer & sing a hymn.

I begin to eulogize him
With all the good times we've had,
All the lyrics we let die unsaid.
He makes of this life a truth confession
Parenting down here both curse & blessing.

I see the undertakers committing ashes to dust
Covering up so much beautiful, the blackness in us
Brown skin & Black dreams like demons within
In a plot my ancestors paid for way back then

Posterity gone & when he's finally home
I still cannot . . . sleep.

This life won't let me hold my peace.
This love a lullaby I sing & repeat.

Asunder

       Too many folk
Sleep well tonight,
       While blood lines streets
In crimson light.

       I pray they don't
Kill my Black son
       Cause I won't rest
Till day is done.

You People

I am unsettled
when I hear privileged you
equate it all to nothing,

Painting smiles where tears have fallen
on what we know & have seen
lived & laid down for.

All the fathers are white,
all the mothers are black
buried, hanging, drenched in the blood of sacrifice.

Your silence screams loud,
kills more than any Chicago
with all its guns.

Freedom Ride

White folk ain't scared
Of people who look like them,

Dress like them, act like them,
American-like, like them—

But with your kinky hair & tennis shoes,
Your untold truths, dark shades & hues,

You're a country bum, a city slicker,
A suburban disturbance, a no-count nigger.

You walk away with both hands up.
Still, you lie drenched in blood & cuffed.

You sit behind a steering wheel
& wake up next to Emmitt Till.

This bus ain't on the road
Toward freedom.

Ritual Combat

Their hands
The color of spilled seed,

Reach up into our wombs
Snatching memories
       that might have been boys,
       who might have become men,
       who might have been answered prayers
Like Samuel to thee.

Fathers to forgotten queens like Sheba—
       planted one night between Samson's & Delilah's
       by laws that break marriage beds in two
       with two hands withholding,
       with shoving all about this holy place,
       this sacred space

Where halves come to make whole
The trampling of men to hallowed grounds,
Turning insides out to harlots,
Releasing souls to prison guards,
To graveyards.

Like Kunta Kinte,
       lifting baby to sky,

We gave you back to God
       for second chances
       for rituals
       for rites
       for truth
       for life.

I Am Not Ashamed of Your Gospel

for the Wintergreen Women

We are connected, henceforth & forevermore by irons binding our fathers & mothers, stowed away in the darkness of a slave ship, bought & sold by evil that still sells all of this. We are kindred spirits kindling spiritual fires, bearing, somehow, pain, summoning, somehow, hope, writing what angels have tried to spell, what root doctors have tried to heal & reverse, what white historians have dispelled to rehearse. Descending on all kinds of division, multiplying every protest, adding to us power, we are ones, the only ones, all the ones we have ever waited for. You wrote the blessed words, you led the sad songs, penned the she psalms, all the prayers for Black women—you prayed them, anointed oil that blessed our pages through pain. Together we have been lonely & alone a proverb dripping from a Harlem wall pipe in the stillness of the cold, the deathbed of the night, you cried freedom from your womb for ours. I am not ashamed of your gospel, for it is Black & female & powerful—an education we need, a hymnal from which we sing. the hope God gave for all the colored girls to save.

To Black Fire

We congregate in mental secrecy
lifting ancient gourds to sky,
grateful for words that fell
from beneath Gabriel's wings:
untitled poems, protests, songs
—revolutions of dead gurus
in between heavens & hells,
souls issued out, offered up,
reigniting fires birthed & burned,
ancient antiques, broken vessels
hanging from Southern trees,
scrubbing red blood from lily white hands,
calloused black feet,
recording rages of the ages,
preaching, scribing, reviving, & baptizing
in the name of justice,
sent from Eden to raise the dead
from ignorant, poisoned dreams,
summoning hues of Blacker blues
with lyrics & syncopated truths,
anointing blank pages with oil
from the inkwells of martyred kings.

This Religion

This twisting of esophageal matters,
This forceful overseeing of lambs,

This coat of unnecessary colors,
This abandonment of green pastures,

This anatomy of chaos,
This politics of a Judas kiss,

This second death without a second coming,
This moneychanger who keeps building new temples.

Birthing Blackness

It's biblical—
We're a van Gogh
Painted over by Jacob Lawrence
On a Sunday morning,

A rapture where
Two souls come to find more
Than rest from generational curses.

Your gift like will—
Ripped open & growing,
Escaping & flowing freely from my womb,
Running rampant, wild & free,

Brought here bequeathing
What the universe gave:
Your own meter, your own rhythm,
Your own beat, your own drum.

Conjuring & summoning up new vines
That sprout & spread like truth fire
In the dark of a white lie,

Resisting a tempo like time,
Reflecting a call like mine.

With All This Freedom

Somewhere up from bravery
You came seeking the promise,
Seeking the promise,
Just seeking the promise,
The promise giver gave—

Blue blood stained & bleeding
From your jugular vein,
Like a wasting of too much time,
A wasting of too much,
Wasting too much
TIME.

A skilled but killed spirit,
A runaway slave
Dead in our living room,
Dead in our living,
DEAD
In our living room—

Where we pray & sing
Where we dream our American dream

Outraged
Out raged
OUTRAGED!

With all this freedom.

My Blackness

I'm not from any side of the town railroad track,
But every moment of my life, I knew that I was black.

My Mama was black, my Daddy was *too*.
I was black at church, even *blacker* at school.

When my blackness walked in at the little country store,
It stopped white conversations overhead outside the door.

White kids knew my name; some even laughed and played.
But my blackness was not allowed at their parties where they stayed.

My blackness has had to rise to every glorified occasion.
Excelling high or performing live, my blackness was the motivation.

My blackness has met conflict in the average public place,
At the local supermarket, on the average white face.

I've been denied opportunities, involved in protests & fights,
Because my blackness was a barrier, not a guarantor of equal rights.

Disappearing Black

It's dying day,
Something like surreal,
Something like coral
Embracing freedom & flowing,
Floating all around.
    You,
Like an heirloom,
Lost in a flood,

Like a slave castle
Burned down,
Carried afar off
To some *damn* nation
Burning bright
With hell,
Light casting on Till's,
Trayvon Martin's,
& Philando Castile's.
    Nobody—
Not a saint, not a sinner,
Not a soul to save you.

Abomination(s)

Mama said this about bull-daggers.
They were *shame n' scandal*
      —something to carry down in history
She'd grab my little hand, hurry on by
      —like the lesbianism—
Somehow, I'd inhale it,
    get it
In my central nervous system
      and die.

Simple Sentences

What was is.
You died in September.
It took three months instead of five.
You saw God outside the picture window.
He stood and cried with me.
The rain was cold.
I grew numb.
The rain poured.
It was, somehow, cleansing.
My face disappeared in a cloud.
I searched for Him.
You left with him.
It was a big black car.
I wrote it down.
I remember.
My heart stopped.
You died.

Mama Was a Negro Spiritual

She was a goodnight prayer,
A moon that shined down
Through my bedroom window.
She was the alphabet, a Sunday
School verse, a third Sunday
Gospel song to rehearse, a mostly
Misunderstood exchange of power,
Responsibility & COMMAND.

She was a black '73 Ford LTD,
A Nottoway River crossing, a house filled
With too many other folks' children,
An orphan that life & death left behind to
Find, to give, some joy. She was a funeral going,
Everybody in Southampton County knowing,
Bad manner destroying pillar of strength.
She was a Friday evening ride to town,
A Saturday morning cleaning, a Sunday
Go-to-meeting kind of human being.
She laughed louder than Jim Crow's law
& cried softer than God's peace.
She was the secret I never told, the carrying
Of some other man & woman's *burden*.
She was rare, uncut, Black & picked up,
Ripped from some earthen mine, placed
Beneath a sharecropper's kind to bear witness,
To bear it all deep down inside.

She was a black hearse, a deaf man walking,
A raising & waving of tired hands.
She was thunder, she was lightning,
A heavy rain that fell in spring.
She was a third-grade education, small-town
Syndication. Her house a good book & she the
Words penned fervently, permanently on all its pages.
She was a Ridley Road scholar, a kitchen
Where cooking got done & well.
She was Mrs. Shirley, the lunch lady, bus driver,
Sammy's wife, giver of too much self.

Mama was a Negro spiritual, a hymn hummed
From inside a Baptist Hymnal, in an old rocking
Chair from a corner of our living room.
She was a wisdom no man could whistle,
A fancy no woman could fake, a journey
None living in the now could take.
She was an old-fashioned lyric
Everybody could lift their voice and sing.

Black Boys

For so many of our brief years,
We built hopes on dreams, energetic & smart,
Gifted with heart, so much passion,
Too much love for life.

But our lives were cut short, our teen-aged,
Black, manhood cut too short, too soon;
It is impossible to realize any more the dream,
To fearlessly hoodie up our heads in winters,
To walk Southern, American suburbs in springs
Without threat to any man or beast,
Just kids with candies, sodas & iced teas.

There will be no junior & senior proms for us,
No caps & gowns, no senior portraits,
No pomp & circumstance for all to see,
No new excitement, no reservations,
No going off to a college city or town,
All plans & promise of higher education shot down.

Our every dream, our hope & wish,
Too many times have come to this,
Black boys overtaken, historically & repeatedly
Mistaken by the darkness,
Left dead, robbed of life in our infant beds by a
Jim Crow that keeps rising from the racist dead,
Our young, black, innocent blood to shed.

Profiled

Down here where ghosts freely ride
They dress up in their Daddies' white hoods,

While blackness rocks our bones to sleep
You can't dream unchained & unashamed,

Un-addicted & free, where spirits spell
Naked truths & new words allow its repeating,

Down here where "this little light o' mine"
Can't shine & nobody's flower forces its way

Up through concrete, barriers, gray matters,
White areas where morning begets mourning

& tears dry up surrounding youth,
Like etchings & hieroglyphs documenting

Pain, a hurt deep down, festered & stained,
Down here where words don't move a soul,

In capsules of life & death, little, big brown
Hands folded methodically, neatly,

In their alabaster boxes, profiled
From A to Z, from America to thee.

Birth of a Sensation

They have no revelation
What's between them and us,
How they're born civic & evil.

    They think it's a jewel.

Shining like diamonds,
      Bleeding like rubies,
           Burning like sapphires.

They let him take US home
Bury US with history,
Beneath heirlooms & Macy's.

They watch him grab it,
Fling dollars at it,
Call it bad names

    Make America hate again.

Primary Colors

In kindergarten,
        They saw them but never used
        Them or picked them up

To color inside
        The lines, maybe to connect
        Dots. Everybody,

They chose the others:
        Greens, blues, violets & reds,
        Browns—at Thanksgiving,

Even whites. Never
        Blacks, because even
        At five, six & seven

In the old Jerusalem,
        Inside the box,
        Black was still black.

What We Might Have Been

What we might have been
Had we not been targets
Shot & left for paper dead,
Convening to converse,
To study & rehearse
This book of sacred words,
Old philosophies marking time,
Moral threads quilting paradigms.

What we might have been
Had we not been damned
To bear this cross,
Emancipated to be emasculated,
Experiencing white like evil,
Being black blood spilled,
Sacrificial lambs slaughtered
In worship of old idols.

What we might have been,
Halves to make worlds whole,
Come just as we are,
Martyred & gone—
Buried between bullets & dreams,

> *reaching for King,*
> *reaching for kingdoms,*
> *reaching for God.*

Here in the Darkness

Here in the darkness,
We keep right on standing up,
Fists raised, hands chained & cuffed.
This God-forsaken darkness
Bleeding us of love & guts,
Videos roll then get cut.

Here in the darkness,
We relive the dreams
Slave rebellions birthed.
This God-awful darkness
With picket signs painted in blood,
A draped coffin & black hearse.

Here in the darkness,
They keep right on killing us,
Not reaching, not policing us.
This unprotected darkness,
It keeps filling up, building up.
It keeps stealing us.

Here in the darkness,
We keep fighting, we keep uniting
Till we are slain
Till we are sane—*no more.*

Hidden Figures

We've been undressed
By ailing eyes,

Evil lips that
Smiled with the wetness
Of dirty tongues,

Smearing families into
Secrecy—

Wretched hands
Plucking us
In forbidden places,

Left to conjure up
This courage—

Prying open
Every shut eye
To this bleeding.

Left Behind

Like black burdens bleeding white hurt,
We are tossed in despair
Finding our way through wretchedness.

We are tears—
Colliding in darkness,
Lighting up poverty
In these places of otherness.

Once hallowed ground,
Naked & barren,
Lodged between heaven & hell,
Seeking to suckle honey
From bitter places,
From pain we excavate.

Old dry bones,
Untold stories & undeveloped negatives,
Pictures the old folk posed for & took
Ancient civilizations—

Left behind.
Left for dead.

Exegesis

For every omen sleeping in a scroll
Encrypted in a timeline, coined

By repressions of deoxyribonucleic acid
Pilfering through light years of cultic

Dissonance obsolete & discovering chaos
Resurging new world order, life

Water toxic with the ancient of ways
Mystified, purified, carbon-dated

Filaments, fragments & species abandoned
To roam uncharted jungles reimagining

Reinventing reality, every other god, every
Other grace, learning just how not to

Un-prepare a place, masculinity, femininity
A desecration of hallowed sounds

How to taste the new wine, envision the first miracle
Purchase the unleavened bread poisoned

With another namesake, kept alive to be crucified
To lie dormant & then fortune-tell it all

In the sleepwalk to unknown glory, how a necessary
Tomorrow may never come.

Down the Red Road

Come look for me, falling from country limbs,
Floating upward to painted skies.
Don't just stop & stare, view my cross briefly.
Walk your dogs along dirt roads toward truth
Where Madame C. J. Walker laid her head
In the hands of time.

Queen of a dirty South,
Keeper of black dreams,
Traveling this road to freedom,
From hell to glory's yonder.
This undated place,
Abandoning the slaves' song,
The backward birthing of babies,
The stolen souls of kings.

Born to bear the burden of strange fruit
Replenishing a barren Eden
Restoring heirs & heiresses
To theocracies—

Where creeds lead the way
Concerned with those who matter
More than idols
More than this world cares
Or cares to fathom.

Intersections

A thing come to past, sometimes to last,
        cymbals smashed too soon,
a Harriet Tubman lynched by noon,
a heaven wind that missed earth,
a Jesus child without virgin birth,
a bald eagle shot down,
a freedom song unsung unfound,
a dark people strung & hung,
a white people laughing, looking on silent,
a swarm of witches circling
        come to devour our nothing left.

They Don't Give a Damn About Us

Except those who feel sorry for us,
        Those who want to be us, or those

Who need us *still*. Every now &
        Then somebody needs a Negro

Woman, man, boy, or girl to serve
        A dinner, a purpose, a summons,

Notice, to make a statement, to take
        A stand, to take a fall, to fall in love

With, to love & to love them back,
        To feed, clothe, shelter, to greet them,

Converse with them in black, to love
        Them with a stereotype, to be a black

Eraser to erase history, misogyny,
        Murder; they need the colored black

In all our exotic, chaotic, chronic &
        Talented hues to dance a jig or sing

The blues. They like us to entertain
        Them, to play a sport or play a role,

They bring us to the table so we can
        Sell ourselves out & short, so we can

See them live. They come for us to convert us,
        Civilize us, help them wrap their heads

Around that which has killed, still
        Kills, and will kill us at random &

At will, so long as we both shall live;
        They need answers, the black experience,

Somebody to make them feel un-ambivalent,
        Entitled, intelligent, more than a US public

School miseducation or fieldtrip; they
        Need a slave narrative, an overstatement,

An understatement, a glimpse of what
        The whole world hates, and if they're so

Kind, to wonder why. They need a Black
        Friend, to signify, to be their alibi, to

Protect with their *savior more than life*
        To me complex. They need a go-to Black

Friend who makes them feel hip, less
        Privileged, more open-minded, to

Un-justify the injustice, to be equal
        In board rooms, fair in court rooms,

Patient, inclusive, & loving in classrooms.
        They come seeking pathways into the

Blackest communities to buy & sell
        Products—their liquors, their loans, their

Drugs, their guns, their ignorance, their
        Prostitution & violence. How can you give a

Damn about a people's revolution who
        Have, for life, been excluded from your

Declarations, your institutions, your
        Religious ideology & your constitution.

You Who Stand

Keep standing all you good Americans who can't
*Under*stand this blackness, this burnt man, this raped

Womanhood, ashes floating in & out of time, bad times,
Antebellum & northern times as we're liberated to be

Lynched again elsewhere beneath streetlights, blue lights,
Media-turned-mafia, Hollywood lights, where thirsts for

Billions leave what you have called niggers under water
Fishing for quarters because America made a *fucking* wish.

We have these pennies in our pockets, but underneath
We are all bronze. In winter, we are warmed by gods &

Dreams of nooses about our necks. We carry a shine
That burns through darkness every time you come

For us, dressed in hatred, slavery, privilege & patriotism.
We are not lazy; we are not crazy. This is not a dream

Some wannabe king had. This shit is real. Everyday a
Lynching, every day a mission, every day we come nursing

These wounds, telling this truth, bearing this burden,
Crying these tired tears, building ground & boiling

Blood while they target our innocent sons like Trayvons
Kill our Sandra Blands with their filthy white hands

While they disrespect 65-year-olds in Georgia's
Alpharetta. Damn you America and every one of you

Who stand, watching as we suffer, watching as we cry,
Watching as we kneel for those of us who die.

Help My Unbelief

Do you know—
How to follow the leader
      like a kindergartner
      like a churchgoer
      like a Trump supporter

How to join all things in life
Together—
      like a puzzle
      like a dysfunctional or blended family
      like a corrupt country.

How to call things
That be not—as though they were
      like peace
      like a blessing
      like gods?

Columbus, Half-mast

He
Looks
Like people
I know—all white
All tight-lipped, slick
Nose big as Black men's
White eyes wide shut with pain
Stealing & discovering the unknown
The innocent blood of mothers
Fathers & children
On his white hands
Sailing.

Mirrors

I am like a stone;
        uncharted, forty-something, strong-willed, creative & free—

I look into a mirror & there she is—
        a young mother wrapping me in swaddling clothes
        giving me to a higher calling, like a Black baby Jesus.

I look closely—
        outside, I see one grandmother, inside another.
        I hear the battle cry; my loins are girded with their honor.

In a different lifetime—
        I am these iron women with their iron men,
        same kind of children, same kind of heart,
        same kind of white folk, same kind of god.

She Who Gives Love

Slayed in a riverbed, captive
by the art of revolution, beauty draped
across jagged edged, sword severing
other men's souls

Sun and moon lie about it all
everything of wonder in orbit
inner cry, a range of mountains
sometimes death

Try them on with grace
cast them off with clarity
She who gives love
must learn to organize pain.

The Invocation

O come
    magnify this white power with me;
Let us exalt its *aim*
    together.

In the antebellum South
    were many mansions;
If it were not so,
    we would not have told you.

They go
    to prepare a place for you,
That wherever slavery is,
    there ye may be also.

O taste & see that *this* slavery is good;
    its mercy—never lasting.
Its truth enduring,
    even into future generations.

What Fools Want

They want warm bodies,
anybody & ask for
No thing in return.

They want to hold worlds,
watch a living thing bow down
To praise them, crave them.

They want blood that keeps
the lamb, earth that keeps the ground,
The mind that keeps you.

Haiku for the Ancestors

      Joy in collard greens,
hope in New Years' black-eyed peas,
      love in all that ain't.

      Sundays stayed holy
singing, cooking, worshipping
      god in those Black hands.

Pledging

We've pledged allegiance
    to flawed beings,
to creeds & colors,
    republics without meaning.

We've created temples
    devoid of gods,
birthed generations
    of malnourished hearts.

With a universe
    of life robust,
we keep choosing
    the death of us.

In shared space,
    we stand displaced
like we're not of
    this human race.

No place on Earth
    to call our own
till six feet under
    cement & stone.

Strong as a Freedom Song

Necessary as a healing, a memorial day flag—a tributary kneeling. On a killing field, your knee is strong as a freedom song. Your hands hold a rock ready, stoning those yet un-accused. A new Jim Crow threatens, while you, a new Negro, shall not be moved. There's a multi-million-dollar joy in standing up for innocence persecuted, for all the martyred men, women & children with a single month to praise them.

After four hundred years, the beat goes on, blue lights descend on blackness with red demons terrorizing the audacity of hope, the audacity of a white dream. You are sacrificial to stand, notable to kneel, honorable to open up this can of 'we are tired of the
world watching as they whip us to death.

What tomorrow brings has been written in a scroll. If 'God loves a cheerful giver,' God also loves a cheerful giver of truth & justice. Carry this torch we carry & watch them come with fire hoses to extinguish the flame of freedom because you, like a prophet on a crucifix, are strong enough to raise the issue of the dead.

Job 1-21

I.

You better be Emmet-Till-still
in that schoolhouse
> till that teacher finish teaching
> till I get home from work
> till I come outta this store
> till I see this white man about a job
> till I pay on this doctor bill
> till I get my hair pressed & curled
> till the choir finish singin'
> till the deacons finish prayin'
> till pastor finish preachin'
> till the insurance man leave
> till I go see the landlord
> till the Supremes go off
> till I'm done sleepin'
> till grandma finish cooking
> till your daddy come back
> till you grown
> till Jesus come.

Job 1-21

II.

Don't you shake your hips
    don't you part your lips.
don't you lift your head
    to look at no white man.

Hold your peace, watch your tongue
    look at the ground, your days be long.
step aside, let white folk pass
    sass the white man, t'will be your last.

Job 1-21

III.

      The black woman giveth
and the whole world taketh away
          blessed be the fruit of her loins.

      The black man buildeth
and the whole world diggeth his grave
          blessed be the power of his sword.

Eulogy for Nat Turner

haiku for Rev. Nathaniel Turner
—leader of the 1831 Southampton County Slave Revolt

We swear to tell it
The whole truth, the Black truth—so
Help these white folk's god

We was all just slaves
Way down here in Southampton
All cross Virginia

All through this here South
We gots tired of being owned
by Turners n' Moores

By de Travises
Bruh Nat—he had seen the light
The only way out

Stuck in a system
Of white men & dey power
Damned to hell on Earth

Field work 'n life 'neath
White folk's feet, dey god's bible
It won't never right

To own nobody
Keep em from a decent life
From buildin' up hope

Snatchin' every right
From Black men, women, children
'Cause we is colored

Just because dey could
Owning folk like property
Buyin', sellin' em.

Then separatin'
Breedin' em, beatin' em down
Work em half to death

In de cotton fields
Walkin' hind a mule 'n cart
Just cookin', cleanin'

In de massuh's house
Usin' de Black woman for
Nursin' white babies

Might as well be dead
Might as well we die trying
To get some freedom

Even if we die
We free from de chains, we free
From shame, from white men

Dey don't care about
Slavin', rapin', 'n lynchin'
No 'nigger' folk here

So why we care 'bout
Killin' who keep slavin' us
With dey religion

I believe a god
Who wants Black folk free, a god
Who b'lieves in me

We wants dignity
We deserves it—by 'n by
So Bruh Nat took it

He won't gon' study
No war no more; he waged it
He fought to be free

That's what Bruh Nat did
He hung, he bled, he died to
Set us, lil' more, free.

Castrated

The amount of Black life gone
From the Black communities
Where love was cultivated
In brilliant, tender hands like
A George Washington Carver's
Killed by eco systemic
Greed breeding color lines of
Hate without local, state, or
National debate. Negroes
Killing Negroes with weapons
White klansmen keep on selling
Drugs white pharmas keep baking
Locked away each day by laws
Racism keeps creating
No cry for no help from no
White man, lest the trap he set
Come for his clan—crystallized
Like meth, like Black diamonds with
Balls from Rough Neck, USA.

Salt

It's hard—not to   sift
    salt
        in wounds   of alabaster
  where devils carve only
lies
When these   worlds   withholding
    nothing
        have their   way
with mother &   with   seed
    with all the igneous
    indigenous   black earth
we are
When caucus   worms come
    feasting
       on whole   souls
  with whole sins
    with whole saints
sapping at the root
          trapping all the truth
When the universe   should   have
    killed
   it has   craved, it has   caved
    with a saving
    grace
   sparing   souls
on days   that   don't seem
   holy.

How to Bury Your Mama

—after Lauren K. Alleyne

You take her hands in yours & you bury them beneath the white sheet that covers her face & yours. You watch her strong Black body slide into the back of a black hearse parked in the grass of her front yard outside the picture window she cleaned for 35 years, your whole life.

You go back into the house & stare at all the empty spaces she once filled: the kitchen where soul food was cooked every single day. Dumplings, cobblers, collard greens, banana puddings, pies & homemade rolls—never to be made again.

You stand in the bedroom where the mirror's edge is decorated all around with pictures of you & your family, where the scent in the curtains she ordered from Sears have instantly increased their worth by millions.

You sit in her old wooden chair with the pillow for cushion & read every letter you wrote to her; you see all the pictures of happy moments you shared, Christmas & birthday cards, your first book—all tucked away in a drawer like stacks of cash she was setting aside for tough times.

You peruse the obituaries of family & friends, grandparents, great aunts & uncles, piled neatly signifying Black death & Black grief, Black love & Black wealth, the best & saddest funeral songs & soloists, a circle of life documenting history, a Black library.

You look at your Daddy, 89 with Alzheimer's, trying to figure out where she is, why Engram's boy took her away in that black car of his because she is not dead, where they laid her & you wish, for a moment, that you could not remember, like him.

You remember the old folk & the Bible saying how quickly we would all be changed. "In the twinkle of an eye," she left the house in a wind that blew, her last breath.

You look at all the people, all the pictures, all the things she wore & touched & you touch them, drape them all over you in hopes of feeling the warmth of her sun again. She is absolutely everywhere: in old sweaters, hairbrushes, pillow shams & in a black leather Sunday School change purse filled with bobby pins.

You still see her. Even in all the faces that are not hers, you see her trying to survive, trying to breathe, trying to find words, spirituals & hugs, motherless children, and god in this medium between Courtland & glory; you want to go with her.

You plan a home going. You decide what & who is good enough to display her worth, to say the right words, to play the right music, to sing the right songs by which men, women, children & a whole community will remember her forever.

You sit in a Black church because a Black church is who she was & you watch people pass by you to view what little remains. You imagine she is somewhere with two wings flying high among angels, singing gospel, cooking & taking care of all the dead children who got their wings too soon, smiling in a heaven as you sit all bereaved & broken trying to exegete scripture, to decipher god—wishing she would just walk in, that it is all a dream, that she is the Lord's next big miracle to be raised from the dead at Shiloh.

You are declared numb, stung by the sting of cancer, left behind with too much to bear, people she loved who, two by two, march behind clergy & casket to a grave she bought, for she believed in preparing a place for her own self.

You melt as the Black preacher speaking blessings over the living & the dead pours ashes that are not hers into a grave that is; you wish everything you ever learned about death was a lie.

In the days, months & years ahead, you hold on to every word she said like it was gospel because she was the only truth you ever knew; you know that now. You do not agree with death; you do not understand god.

You take her hands in yours & you bury them beneath the white sheet that, eventually, covers all.

Stars of Wonder

Stripped from a canvas in the cosmos,
We survive in halfway houses, halfway

In houses, half-alive, half-gone, half-wed,
Half-white, half-pretty, half-dead, dropped

From skies to count what never adds up, just
Us tending to the live roots of every lynching

Tree, never climbing, never climaxing, never
Completely in or of our right minds, false

Like a cow jumping over the moon, like a slave
Master's Jesus coming to save us real soon.

Zip Code: 75215

Asleep in this grave
Black, alone & silenced by
White people with guns

Uniformed & veiled
We sing, praise, worship & hug
These Americans

Wipe their shame away
Judas kiss ourselves to hell
Righteous forsaken.

America

    There's so much hell here,

Black lives, Black tears, Black matters,

    White falling from sky.

Legend of Southampton County

Of Cross Keys and Dismal Swamp, few
know where this antebellum American history lies.

'Tis black, white, and red—all over,
mulatto babied, bastard child, back woods, where
the Nottoway River still runs. Hidden like
a slave's sword, like a soldier's Bible,
in a Virginia clearing of things unholy.

Latorial Faison is an African American poet, author, professor, and veteran senior military spouse from rural Southampton County, Virginia. Faison completed a BA in English with a minor in Religious Studies at the University of Virginia, a Master of Arts in English at VA TECH, and doctoral studies in Education at Virginia State University. Her writing explores Black Southern traditions as well as the intersections of race, culture, and identity.

Dr. Faison, a Pushcart nominee, has been awarded fellowships from The Association of Writers & Writing Programs (AWP), Virginia Humanities, and the Furious Flower Poetry Center. Her poetry and creative nonfiction have been anthologized and published in *Callaloo, Obsidian: Literature & Art in the African Diaspora, PRAIRIE SCHOONER, West Trestle Review, AUNT CHLOE, Artemis Journal, The Southern Poetry Anthology, About Place Journal, Southern Women's Review, RHINO, Deep South Magazine, Stonecoast Review, Solstice, Poetry Quarterly, Virginia's Best Emerging Poets, Cultural Homefront, Penumbra*, and award-winning books *Three Minus One* inspired by the film *Return to Zero*, and the NAACP Image Award winner *Keeping the Faith: Stories of Love, Courage, Healing, and Hope from Black America*. Faison has edited and published junior writing anthologies in both fiction and poetry in collaboration with military-serving schools and community organizations in Virginia.

A recipient of the Tom Howard Poetry Prize, Faison has been a finalist for the CAVE CANEM Poetry Prize, the Louise Bogan Poetry Award, and the North Street Book Prize. She is the author of poetry books, *Mother to Son, I Am Woman, flesh, LOVE POEMS, Secrets of My Soul, Immaculate Perceptions*, and the Amazon Kindle best-selling trilogy collection *28 Days of Poetry Celebrating Black History*. Faison is also the author of education research, *The Missed Education of the Negro: An Examination of the Black Segregated Experience in Southampton County, VA, 1950-1970*, and books for young readers, *Kendall's Golf Lesson* and *100 Poems You Can Write*. She is a Life Member of the historic Wintergreen Women Writers Collective and The Poetry Society of Virginia.

Faison's Pulitzer nominated and best-selling poetry collection, *Nursery Rhymes in Black*, won the 2023 Permafrost Poetry Book Prize and was published by University of Alaska Press in 2025. She currently serves on the faculty at Virginia State University as Assistant Professor of English and Chair of The Department of Languages & Literature. Faison is married to her high school sweetheart, a retired US Army Colonel, with whom she has three sons.

www.ingramcontent.com/pod-product-compliance
Lightning Source LLC
Chambersburg PA
CBHW030056170426
43197CB00010B/1550